TOGETHER ALONE
fragments & poems

written and illustrated by Syrah Kai

Connect & read more at:
Instagram: @syrah.kai
www.syrahkai.com

Together Alone

"Paradoxically, the ability to be alone is the condition for the ability to love."

Eric Fromm, *The Art of Loving*

Syrah Kai

ACKNOWLEDGEMENTS

Thank you to everyone who helped make this possible, from listening to me talk about my writing process, reading my first draft and giving feedback, helping me with technical aspects or just cheering along from the sidelines. There is a group of people I would like to thank specifically for their effort and support in my development of *Together Alone.*

In no particular order I'd like to thank my beta readers; ADD NAMES and my helpful and inspirational friends; AND NAMES who encuoraged me to lean on them, and I'm gateful that I did.

Syrah Kai

NOTE FROM THE AUTHOR

why I wrote this book, what is means, the journey, the overlap, the synopsis, the invitation to dive in, digest and meditate on the images and poetry etc etc

Everything starts with an intention, and I would like to reveal my own behind this collection of poems and the creation of *Together Alone*. It started as a thought that flashed through my mind, it was both an idea and an insight. It came to me just as I was completing *Growing Gold*. I was thinking to myself, "We all go through the exact same cycles of transformation, and not just us, everything follows the cycles of death and rebirth. Yet we never know what stage someone is in, or if we are sharing a mutual experience. It feels so ubiquouts but so special, so rare. These individual expriences of the cycles that are literally everywhere. We are togther alone in this, always."

Together Alone stayed with me from that late summer day in 2019 and I started exploring what that meant to me, and what it meant relative to the Everyone and the Everything. It was pure synchronious luck that as I began to deeply meditate on the nature and realities of togetherness and aloneness that a pandemic swept the world forcing populations to retreat. Typically I am quite the hermit, despite the extroversion and volume I can reach, I prefer to stay in and read or hole up in my office and play with cretivity. It's not everyday that a hermiting poet writing about the pain and comforts of company and solitude gets to witness the world go through the stages of death and rebirth quite literally together, quite literally alone.

But as unicersal is the cycle of death and rebrith, as is this axis between the other and the me. And while the pandemic proved to be a great catalyst in the gestation of this book I do not explicitly call out the virus. Instead I go down the memory lanes we all went into as we spent days inside, with nowhere to be, the memories of childhood, relationships, regrets, and the periods where I had felt

8

Syrah Kai

CONTENTS

Together Alone

TOGETHER

TOGETHER ALONE

No matter how isolated
you think you are
you're not the only one
suffering

we share this experience
the highs and lows
we are always connected
together alone

CAN WE COME TOGETHER

Can this be a remedy
to combat the case of the common
cluttered condition of existence
for when you have a tickle in your throat
that makes you want to throw
your hands in the air and scream

I GIVE UP
TAKE ME NOW

can we remember the connections
that hold us together
so we don't fall apart
and embarrass ourselves
in the eyes of god?

can we care, just enough?
can we carry the burden of freedom
without bearing the cross?

can we forgive without permission?
can we let go after a day of meetings, nonstop?

can you look at yourself in a store window
and see how the sun bends to your body—submitting
can you show the same mercy?

can you see yourself in the stars?
can you be one drop in the ocean
and still know who you are?

MORE KINDS OF TOGETHER

So what if there's a million kinds
of loneliness
there are more kinds of together
than you'll ever know
more languages of love
and colours of affection

there's long conversations
followed by acceptance
there's mistakes that can still be forgiven
like the lies that can't be untold
there's giving without needing
and sharing warmth when it gets cold

united by simply existing
know that you're never alone
even when it feels like it
especially when you feel it most

NEVER ALONE

They say you are born alone
and die alone
but they always forget one thing,
what about our mothers?

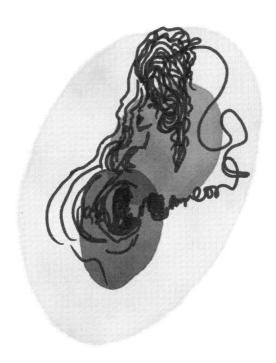

WE MAY BE
INDIVIDUALS NOW

BUT WE WERE ONE
NOT˄ LONG AGO
   TOO

UNIVERSAL DONOR

We belong together
in the most pathetic of ways
for life, for love,
food and shelter
helpless we are
without the sympathy of each other
we can't function as islands
so we do what we can
and import the rest

we can hate ourselves
as much as we want
honk with rage, tell screens to shut up
live to anger, get angry about love
we can waste our time
fighting over the moon
with silly human guns

but no matter what
at the end of the day
when the churning gets tough
we always belong together
for life, for love
and so we take the time
to share our precious blood

WE ALL BURN

Some hearts beat
like thunder
booming under
                    pressure
and some are the drops of rain
eroding what is weak
washing it away

some hearts
are the wind
gentle but deceiving

all our hearts
are bloody
from the passion
of yearning

Syrah Kai

WHOLE PEOPLE

We have all questioned
the autonomy of others
are they whole people
can they be trusted?
         (am I to be?)
maybe we aren't different
same fears
same grief
same tempting apathy
I am you
so suddenly

MISSED CONNECTIONS

Right now we need to keep our distance
but all this danger awakens the animal in me
with the threat of sickness,
collapse and upheaval
all I crave is human company, community,
the safety of numbers
a tribe of hunters and lovers
but that will only kill us faster
so I will stay where I am
for as long as I need to
just know that I miss you,
strangers of the world
and I can't wait to walk past you again
eventually

Syrah Kai

FORGETTING WHO WE ARE

Let's not forget that
we are more connected
than we are different
that when given the chance
we will help more than
manipulate for our benefit

let's not forget that
our first instinct is to reach out
and our second is to grab hold
to lift our fallen as was done for us before

let's not forget that we are each other
calling to say
hey how are you doing
I haven't heard from you in days

Together Alone

MAKE THEM HEAR WHAT THEY'VE DONE

Scream your heart out
and cry out loud
make them hear what they've done

force them to feel a semblance of anything
except greedy and numb

let the world know what is really going on
send me a sign

blink twice if they have a gun

22

THE OTHER WOMEN

Halfway across the world
and very close to home
there is a girl
who has never made a decision
of her own
her father tells her who to be
and her brother watches her oblige
she is passed from man to man
until she is suited
with a husband
and to him she serves
but for her children, she lives
her life is not her own
she is just a beautiful inconvenience

WORK OF LOVE

It's more than a chakra opening
it is an intricate dance constantly changing
one day you lead
the next day it's me
it's work and worry
hidden in layers of homemade buttercream icing
it's late night talks about aliens and philosophy
and then later nights confronting our dirty laundry
like my bad habits, your biggest fears
and like dirty laundry
it's never done, never fully clean
love is a chore
you must learn to enjoy
because you appreciate nice things
and riches worth keeping
don't come easy

PATIENT YET?

Patience is a lesson
that requires
repetition
you can't be patient
once
and then call yourself
a master
you must face every set back
with the same calm
composure
and be willing to endure

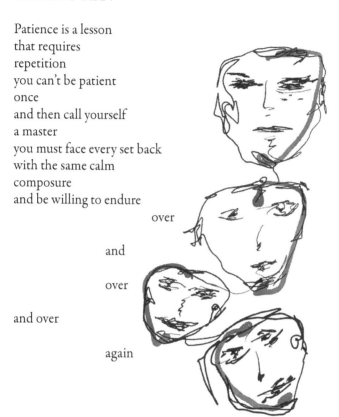

over

and

over

and over

again

SURVIVAL

my survival
is yours

but

your

survival

is not mine

ANYONE HOME?

We refuse to believe
we are alone
so we send rockets and bottles
and balloons with notes
into the vague unknown
desperate to find out
who else calls this universe
home

THE FUTURE IS CANCELLED

The future is frightening
because you never know
when it actually begins
or is actually happening
it stays in a limbo of waiting
for what, for now? for now to end?

I could live in a state of feverish wonder
while the future forever eludes me
but I don't think the future
exists

THE EVERYDAY

But I have to go
there is rain painting the roads
dropping to the ground
making music without any scripted sounds
it just goes
running for the train
another cup of coffee
small talk with baby hairs
I want to make a cozy sweater
out of those rebellious curls
set a new trend
change the world
it's lunch again
and again
and again
go home
push through closing doors
make room! the world is full of other people too
but before my clenched fists can fall off
a concealed furball yawns
hidden in a lap
under a woman's coat
she looks around and pulls it close
but lady,
you know you don't have to smuggle those

29

BELONGING

I need to belong
like I need to breathe

I can breathe alone
but I can't eat

I can eat alone
but I can't speak

I can talk to myself
but I can't feel

I can touch myself
but it feels like nothing

I need to belong to be

THE HERMIT CARD

Ask me my favourite thing to do
and I won't tell you the truth
because the truth is I love to hermit
but it's better kept a secret
alone in me
alone together
living a rhythm of wine and coffee
and afterdark thought trains
that go off the rails and into the wild
entirely unknown
entirely inside me a world
I have built
a garden I've replanted repeatedly
with crows, plot twists,
wind chimes and bees;
background noise because
even when I want to be alone
I need the world around me

LIBRA & ARIES

Opposites attract
to fill in the gaps
the weaknesses we hate facing
they put a spotlight on our shadows
the versions of ourselves
that we could never be

opposites love
to taunt our hearts
and tease our biggest dreams

opposites are us
the other way around
attracted to our individuality

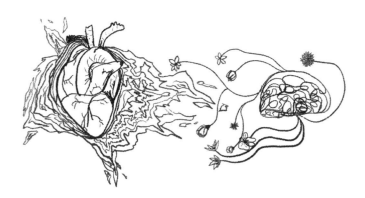

BY ANY MEANS NECESSARY

Sometimes comparison sneaks into the room
unnoticed
it passes through
shakes hands with your idols
and contemporaries
gossips about nonsense
and then tries to hack into your conscience
and tell you it's okay to do
whatever
you have to do

AS FLEETING AS THE CLOUDS

Emotions are big soggy clouds
fading in and
manifesting back out
with a flow that has no pattern
and a chaos that maintains control
feel as it happens
but don't let the meaning go

INFINITE SUN

Watching the sunrise
while the blood rushed
to fill the veins in our eyes
this perfect instance
can only live for a minute
but the depth of the moment
feels so infinite

DISTRACTED DISTRESS

Too busy
living,
breathing,
being
too caught up in the moment
to notice
the world is crumbling
like the end of a ring around a rosie
it's all falling down
but you can't hear the sound
of eerie silence
the calm before catastrophe
when you are so busy
living,
breathing,
being

Syrah Kai

DYING TO DISCONNECT

Disconnection
both a dream
and a nightmare to live in
to be far from the world
and all her worries
but to also be ripped apart
from anything worth loving

TELL ME WHAT YOU NEED

So tell me
what is really going on
under your skin
because I don't trust the outside
looking in
I know there is something in there
you are keeping hidden

if you need to unfold
it is safe to do so
I can be the blanket you need
wrapped around your shoulders
so you can unfurl and fall out carefully
just tell me

COFFEE AND KINDNESS

Without the kindness of others
strangers and lovers
I don't know if I'd still be alive
to answer Camus' question
coffee or suicide?
a fragment is
this life of mine
yet so precious and essential
we must live with intention
to be good
to survive
to make the world somehow
a little bit more kind

CAUTION: CURIOSITY

There are two kinds of people
those who learned only
by touching a hot stove
and others who chose
not to confront the heat
of their curiosity

DON'T SHOOT

I shot a gun
once
at a range
just for fun

my first shot was hot
the shell went up and
down the gap of
my crewneck sweater
burning my right breast
it sizzled
tsss

but nevertheless
my shot hit the innocent outline
of a stranger
square in the chest

I dropped the gun
and clutch mine
and cried—
I will never shoot again

WHO KNEW

Who knew
emotions had boundaries
and that you could love someone to death
but still need to keep them at a distance
to protect your existence

who knew
saying no was
another way of saying I love you
because if I said yes when I didn't want to
I'd be lying

who knew

NOW YOU KNOW

The real conspiracy
what they truly don't want you to know
the big secret they hide in plain sight
the fine print in the terms and conditions
you signed with shut eyes
is this:

we are in this together
but they want you to feel alone

SPILLING

I want to taste
whatever it is
you are trying
to escape

Syrah Kai

THOUGHTS AND PRAYERS

According to them
it is kind and gorgeous
to feel for the unfortunate
but it's reckless and wasteful
to do what needs to be done

A SOUR DREAM

All the safety nets and survival kits
we built hoping never to need
are now dried up and empty
like the promises we made
to poor immigrant families
lies wrapped like candy
tricking children into never trusting
treating trust like a costume
you can't return after halloween

DIVIDED NATIONS

The world is sorry
for the countries
we used to envy

we are so sorry
that you have to worry
about water that wants to
break your bones
about doctors that have to
tell you no
about teachers who love
out of pocket
for theatre disguised as news
so you watch it

sorry we can't influence your direction
like you have coerced so many of ours
we wish we could wish you all the best
but we know that this is not how it ends

masters must be met
and risen above
freedom must be reclaimed
not given up

sorry this is the way it goes
not sorry to see the people grow

GOOD THING WE LOVE TO LOVE

There are times when
I truly believe
that if it weren't for our love
of being touched
we would have annihilated our species
last century
but lucky lucky
we have time to touch
a little bit longer
before getting back
to destiny

WE ARE ON TIME

Maybe we aren't doomed
as a species
of materialism and stupidity
maybe we are right on time
on cue—on key
to break out into the chorus
of our evolution
maybe we aren't anywhere close
to the end
but actually in the middle
of the great eventually

A CHILD ASKING FOR MORE

I close my eyes and get lost
in the stories hidden behind my skin cells
the oil my grandmother used
to bathe herself
the fruit her mother picked
mint tea and pomegranates
the fish her oldest sister
caught for a late summer supper
a child asking for more
a father sharpening weapons
a child asking for more
cousins giggling about weddings
a child asking for more
I close my eyes and hear their stories
about olives and new cities
I close my eyes and listen
and hear myself
a child
asking for more

APART OF ANOTHER

If they say you're born alone
and die alone
then they are forgetting about our mothers,
they say this stuck inside
their semi sentient bodies
forgetting that even without a team of doctors
and extended family
we can't possibly be born alone
we always come from some body
between cells and birth
she thinks she is alone
in her pain, waiting
but as we take first breath
we are together, living

KARMIC GIFTS

I never felt more present
than when he called me
god's gift
because his family believed
that only the lucky
get daughters first
so as the god of gifts
I will use my first act of mercy
to give you this:
        you did better
        than your dad did

REBORN DAUGHTER

I have been reborn
from the ashes of my mother
I am more than just her daughter
I'm her second chance
and this time
there is less sacrifice
I will work harder than she had to
but I will not work more
because this life isn't just for living
it's for learning and becoming
because my mothers before
couldn't live out loud
so for them I will live
for myself and hope
I make them all proud

HOW DOES SHE JUGGLE EVERYTHING?

I want to take this chance to thank
my mom
for so often leaving her job
in the middle of the day
to pick me up from school because I called
saying I was sick

but truthfully I wasn't

I was just sick of the nonsense,
the other kids,
the words that didn't mean anything,
I was sick in the sense
that you could see it in my eyes
but not feel it on my forehead

thank you for dropping everything
to cater to me
now I have a job and can barely
get away to get my teeth cleaned
I don't know what I would do
if I had a small human
depending on me

thank you
but I still don't know how you juggled
everything

MIDDLE SCHOOL

It's been years since the last pudding cup
was aimed
at the back of my tangled head
it's been over a decade since
the bathroom walls wrote such mean things
about the body I was growing in
there have been several lifetimes since
those halls almost took mine
and to think I almost stopped my heart
because kids couldn't be kind

INTERNET FRIEND

Don't tell anyone, but we met on the internet
before it was okay
back when it was dangerous
and our parents told us not to give out our real names
it's our secret
even till this day
although we never found each other in person
you were a better friend to me
during the worst middle school days

BEGGING TO BE OPENED

I know what they say about the moon
about how she pulls the oceans
and so she must pull on us too
since we are also bodies of water
trapped in sweaty containers
of waves crashing and tides dropping
so my sadness too
sinks then rises
in sync with the steam coming off
the morning mountains
I am a confinement of emotions
like the ocean
begging the moon to break me open

COLONIES INSIDE ME

Each cell must fight
and die
to renew the tissue
of space and time
they charge fearlessly
into the sun
soldiers of many—
yet the sum of
just one

HOLDING ON FOR MY LIFE (DON'T DROP ME)

I have fallen deep
into our feelings
but the part of me that fears this
knows the tragedy is worth it
knows the heart is deaf to sirens
as my grip only tightens
on a hand that feels no pain

LONG DISTANCE CALLING

Do you remember those late night
long distance phone calls that used to last
until my sunrise and your midnight?
I'd whisper in your ear
in my lowest pillow voice
and I could practically feel your warmth on mine
how absurd
we connected through a screen
a collapsed world
the distance was a fallacy
you were here
and it was real

FALLING WITH THE WIND

My love was carried by the wind
like a clever piece of pollen
planted in places I've never heard of
in the pockets of hearts I can't reach
my love found you before fate
could cross paths with me

FROM A DISTANCE

I kiss you goodnight
with weighted eyes
and you wish me good morning
as you yawn into your coffee
this is love
from a distance

CITRUS

I can't eat an orange
without wanting to write a poem
or kiss the back of your neck
ever since you peeled one
slowly, in bed after sex
that citrus fruit has become
my subconscious aphrodisiac

TOUCHED

I refuse to live
anywhere else
but beneath
the weight of your
fingertips

Syrah Kai

'TIL DEATH, THEN PEACE

And when the time comes
for me to die
I will let go
so that love may come back to you
in another form
because only when you are at peace
will I be able to rest too

JEDDO

I know your time is coming soon
to embark into the dead unknown
you've lived long, considering
your little life was war ridden
but then gold stricken

we never shared the same language
but we sure both knew
how to swim the Mediterranean
and spend hours walking with aimless direction

you were a dreamer who had to raise a family
under a bomb
you did everything you could,
and everything else doesn't matter anymore

if you've forgotten my name
it's okay
I still love you, anyway
goodnight jeddo
habibi

FROM THE OTHER SIDE

If I die in my sleep
just know I love every inch of you
and I will find out what's on the other side
do some networking
put in a good word
with that B karma
I'll sit with you in your grief
I'll respect your process of overcoming
but know that
right now
you are the reason I still breathe

you're still here

as long as

I can

remember you

I'M SOFT

I'm soft
in all the ways
you are not
but I don't mind
all the ways
you are rough

UNIVERSAL RESPONSE

what was once
the singularity
    is now the universal

response to the
smell of fall

LIFE ON A PLATTER

It's yours
the sky and the sun and the ocean floors
it's yours
to take and take care of
yours to cherish or destroy
yours to share with others
or squirrel away
because it's yours
so what will you do
with the world the universe
has made you

INEVITABLE PEACE

Thinking about the inevitable
our mortality
together and individually
our relationships will all eventually crumble
as will our bodies
nothing can escape the gravity of infinity
the balck hole that pulls apart our matter and eats our souls
death and heartbreak
pity and despair
different spirals lead to the same dimension
where there is nothing left to touch
or compare

if the universe

made me

like this

you can
accept me

like this

LIFE IS A SPECTRUM

We are bodies built on spectrums
with different capacities to think
                       feel
                       love
we are infinite expressions
of individuals
we are rainbows of hope
that come from wells deep with doubt
but from time to time we cross paths
just so
that we connect instantly
and the spectrum goes on

LISTEN TO THE ODD ONES

Misunderstood souls are not the shadows
of society's selfish goals
they are signs of change about to unfold
and alter the entire human landscape
they are the pushers of reason
the questions of faith
the provocation we need
to take a hard look at our fate
and decide if we want to expire or evolve
will we refuse to be uncomfortable for a little while
or would we rather push the collective along
and entertain that perhaps the sun
orbits something greater
and maybe we are all fluid, loving, creators

STRUTTING

It's completely fine
if you can't relate to my lifestyle
or reasons why
so you can walk in your shoes
and I'll strut in mine

Syrah Kai

GIRLS KISSING

Of all the first kisses I've given
and received
our lip glossed moment
against my parents car
in the dead of January
was more than just practice
before your date at the movies
it was poetry to me

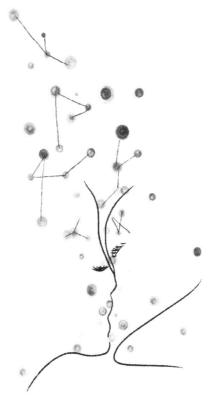

77

WATCH WHERE YOU SPILL

It will take a little more than
some soap and water
to remove the stains
of the unnecessarily hot
tea you made

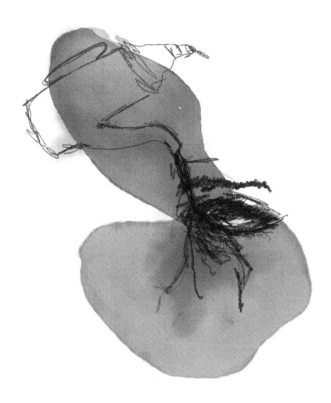

COLLAPSE

These aren't uncertain times
these are times of certain death
    with idols falling
    and leaders digging their graves
these times aren't anything short of obvious
and expected
because who couldn't have predicted
the fall of rome
    when stars get too dense
    they start to implode

so here we go

FOLLOWED HOME TOO MANY TIMES

Followed home by men on bikes
I was young
and apparently ripe

I couldn't leave the house
without unwanted attention
being thrown in my direction

I was ashamed
of my supple complexion

UNITE THE TRIBE

Becoming one is overrated
let's become it all
and defy the rules we created
to unite the tribe,
we must love their hatred

THE LIE

We love—

like nothing else has ever mattered and maybe nothing ever did. Maybe every moment we get depends on what we do with what we have now. And we seem to be passing every test and tumbling into the next. We are a riddle I have no interest in solving. I have to admit, it is a little confusing, this dizzy daily living. One minute I love the world and feel every heart in my own, and the next thing you know I can't stand any living soul because they are so wrapped up in their own untidy worlds and can't see how all the trees come together to make the forest. And that their needs are nothing compared to the health of the ecosystem, the greater good, the whole. It's a confusing state, to be so in love and so drowned in hate. In those spirals I try to remind myself that I am one of them, I too am selfish, I too am flesh I am also crazy, sad and stupid, I make mistakes and forget there's life behind the eyes of the rude passengers and customers. We are all just love drunk dumb struck babies walking around unsuprivised missing our mommies. And as much as I am I, we are all this at the same time and I couldn't separate myself from it all, no matter how hard I try—

the individual is the biggest lie.

IT WAS A DEAFENING ATTRACTION

The tension between us was so loud
I couldn't hear the warnings

TOO BAD WE MET

I never liked how we met
but more than that
I hate how I stayed anyway
how you played with me
how you almost got away
with keeping me down
when I was meant to erupt
through tinted glass ceilings
and into the clouds
I was meant to rain my heart
over everything I touched
but you interrupted my train of thought
I never liked how you loved

LETTING YOU IN

I'm not going to fight the urges this time
the ones that tell me
you might actually be alright
because genuinely I see
life is better
filled with more naps and laughter
with your sweet nonsense
and chest against mine
I think I might
let you in this time

BE TOUCHED FOR ONCE

The truth is
we are all lonely
tired and kind of horny

we are hungry for something
that can't be acquired
we are hunting for a fate
that doesn't leave much to be desired

but our satisfaction
depends more
on all that
can't be
touched,

so fuck it—be touched
be moved
let what you feel
                flow through you
like a net
catching what needs to be saved
just be careful you don't dam
what is yet to be understood
or explained

WHEN TO LET GO

You'd think it would be more sensible
to maintain control

it would be a safer bet
to just stick to what you know

but inner riches
don't come from being solitary

it takes exposure of the senses
to love and envy

and all the lavender and grey
that bleed between polarities

there is wisdom in knowing when
to let go and when to hold on like crazy

TOGETHER WE TAKE FORM

Lonely is shattering into
a million pieces
together is everything
you can make
out of clay

BUTTERFLY FLYING HIGH

Nature lives in a state
of meditation
a calm chaos
that continues to evolve acute awareness
and profound detachment
like the birds who sing songs
that the deep sea creatures
will never hear of

GENTLE GIANTS

Your hands are softer than mine
and sometimes I forget
that even though you're a man
made of mountains
there's a sapling in your heart
I must not neglect

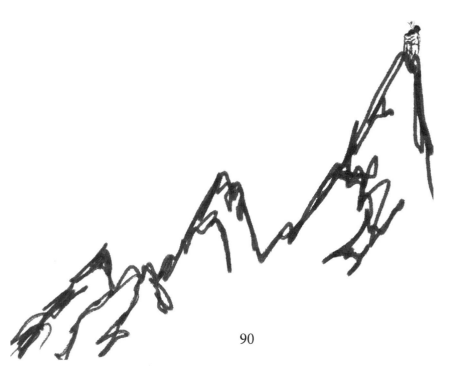

SOFT EYES

Eyelashes love to flirt
they tease and toy
and play all day
whispering about what they will do
to each other
when night finally falls
and sleep overcomes the body
how they will properly embrace
interlocked,
and dream about a love
that flutters freely
and doesn't leave stains
on your face

FIRST COMES CONNECTION

Eye contact
and honesty
come before
ugly laughs

SWEET HEART

Like a mango
I can't peel you
as easily as everyone else
so I'll cut deep into your centre
until I hit rock
and then suck your juices out

IF YOUR HANDS
 FIT MINE
WHY CAN'T WE
 SEE WHAT ELSE
   DOES?
I HAVE A FEELING
  YOU GIVE GREAT
 HUGS
   (AND THEN SOME)

THE COLOURS WE REMEMBER

Orange like the time
you painted my nails
yellow like every afternoon
you napped
while I slowly exhaled
red like the lace I wore
when I made you dinner
and my face after you kissed me
in places that make me quiver

ENDLESS COLLIDING

The last time we got this close
I forgot how to sleep
and they didn't have a word
for what I was experiencing
the gratitude I felt for the sun rising
you surprised my monotony

the last time we did this
I swore it would be the last
but now I want to enjoy
every minute we have while
we dance across our paths
one more memory to never look back

OK FINE, I THINK ABOUT YOU SOMETIMES

If it will help you sleep
then yes
I think about you sometimes

but at the risk of giving you bad dreams
I won't tell you how
I still fantasize
about seeing you sometimes

about how I will look so effortless
and incredible
that your eyes will try to lock mine
as you follow me in a crowd

but I'll have more important matters
and bigger things on my mind
so I won't notice you
or even try

and how that will leave you
feeling itchy with regret
and hot with doubt

so yes
if it will help you sleep at night
I think about you sometimes
but don't get excited
because I don't remember
the last time—
and now doesn't count

RIPPED CURLS

I think about you
when I brush my hair
because it's something you used to do
at the end of a long week
when my curls became matted with dread
now I stare at myself as I rip through tangles
I'm not gentle like you were
and my fingers are lined with lead

I ALWAYS KNEW
YOU'D CHANGE MY LIFE
  BUT NEVER
THIS WAY

ONE OF OUR LAST MEMORIES

Remember when you kissed
the newest freckle
on my chest
I had returned from Beirut
with sun damage
and you couldn't get enough of
the way I blushed
so you bought me something pretty
and said
it would never be enough

Syrah Kai

TALL WOMAN, SHORT MAN

We were just a couple of loners taking on the world
who shared the same taste in music
and a love for one particular artist

we were just two outcasts
from different social classes
me, the swan girl who grew from a tree trunk
into a queen
and you, the small framed man
with heartbreak
on his sleeves

you broke rules to entertain me
and I made your eyes wide and heart crazy
that was another life
but sometimes, not often
I wonder how you're doing

COMPASSION IS A FUNNY THING

So I met your family
and instantly understood everything
I see now, the difference
between what you needed
and what you got as a child
when the hugs stopped
when violence entered
I see the depth of your imperfections
and I need you to know
that there's no other mess I'd want to kiss
no one else I'd want to heal with

A HEART WORTH SHARING

I wish I could clone your essence
and inject it into a dart
I would go around
shooting the heartless
and watch them fall in love
like art

Together Alone

EVERYTHING WE LOVE FITS IN A BOX

I can't tell the difference
between what's yours,
what's mine,
and what was ours
I know the desk belongs to you
and the couch belongs to me
but what are we going to do with the love
we bought together
like the art
and the christmas tree

THIS IS A LOVE THAT NEVER ENDS

There is a deep sadness behind love
this tragedy of a
fall
flushed eyes and sweaty palms
are the signals of imminent pain
that something could take this love
and rip
the peace away

but before we can swear off
our next attempt at love
we catch ourselves forgiving
with eyes closed and arms wide open
with the tipping faith
that this love is different
it won't happen again

SOMETHING A ROMANTIC WOULD SAY

I can't wait until you fall in love,
my dad said to me
while I examined my 14 year old face
noticing new bone structure in the side-view mirror
bye bye baby cheeks

"Why can't you wait?"
I asked, never breaking my own eye contact
because love hurts.
I looked away, at my father's face
"So you want me to be in pain?"
it was rhetorical but he replied anyway

*Yes, I do. It'll hurt and it will be painful but in a
different way. You'll understand when you feel it, and
then you'll learn things that I can't teach you. You'll
grow through the pain.*

I glanced back at myself,
and told my cheek bones to slow down
there's no hurry, I thought
as we pulled into my highschool parking lot
love will find its way

TOUGH LOVE

Tough love
tougher me

I wanted to hold you
but instead I let you sink deep

telling myself
you needed to learn to swim

and that you wouldn't grow
if you depended on my reach

until one day
it was me that couldn't breathe

couldn't scream
couldn't ask for help
or wake myself from this dream

I needed relief but no one could hear or see me
because my cracks were on the inside

and people can't read minds
so no help was received

I had to pick myself up
and try to stand on my own broken feet

tough love
carved a softer me

so if you need a boost
I'll help build the ladder you need

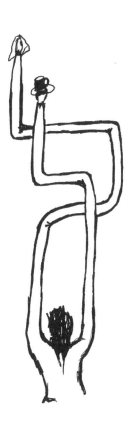

107

YOU DESERVE MORE

I hope life gives you everything
you need
but when you are without
just know
you can call on me

Syrah Kai

BIG TALK

We make small talk
but I know you have a big heart
that secretly wants to dig a hole to jump out
and bleed all over me

Together Alone

I NEED YOU SO MUCH CLOSER

This isn't close enough
your body is in the way
open your chest up
let me scoop your heart like vanilla ice cream
on a hot August day
you're still too far for me to connect with
what are we going to do about all this distance
the barrier between our lips
I want to do more than touch your skin

SOMETHING TO SAY

I'm bursting with joy
I'm falling apart
who can I tell
who can I trust
to protect my bliss (my catastrophe)
when there's tidal waves
I can't tame (for better or not)
hello, my friend
do you exist—
can we talk?

A TEMPT

I could do it all
without you
but I'd like you to join me
there's room if I move
a little this way
there's no pleasure
if I can't share it—
and trust me, there's plenty
please, can I tempt you
                    to stay?

KISSING CELLS

Finally!

We are together on every level
except molecular
finally we are one and two
one for me and one for you
in a pod made just for lovers
we are together, beyond words

YOU ARE HOME

When it comes to us
nothing else exists
we love in a way
that defies the laws of physics
because the heart of matter
is impossible to know
but when it comes to you I trust
this is a safe place to call home

WILD WITH AGE

I always thought you looked better
with laugh lines
and little grey whiskers
because I like watching the way
your beauty takes age
and how you grow into a better version
of all your grandfathers
kiss me with those lips
you got from your mother
and I'll hold you like a child
no matter how old we grow
you always keep me alive and wilder

LOOK AT US

I want us to be the view
they spend so much money
on window cleaners
to better admire

YOUR SOMEONE

Come,

and we can be one
one you've forgotten
the one I let go
the last one
the best one
stop
let me be someone,

yours

A LITTLE NAKED

You told me to take off
the hair band around my wrist
as you unlinked the graduation
chain that had been permanently
installed for years around your neck
you wanted us to be as naked
as we felt
you wanted only me
only me
and nothing else

GREY

How did you know
I loved cloudy days
beacuse truth be told
I can't get over
how good you look in grey
is that you casting skies over
are you fliring with me
by making it rain?
because I forgot my umbrella
on purpose again

TELL ME SOMETHING UNTRUE

Tell me what I want to hear
tell me to stay
tell me you wish I was her
tell me something untrue
so I can have another reason
to find an excuse
to get a little too close to you

GROWING TOGETHER

What is best
and what could be better
are fighting
over my goals
and my attachment
to my lover

BAD WORDS

I've spoken words so hot
they still haunt me
and if I've ever scorned you
chances are

I am still so sorry

DEEP BREATH

If I fall into your arms
I might never resurface
(I don't need air)

I might drown in your delight
I might not have the energy to fight
(I might not care)

if I run through your eyes
I know I'll find something
I know I'll see truth
I know I'll feel pain
(pain I can bare)

if your mouth touches mine
you'll feel my fire
(and I'll melt your stone)

you'll hear my secrets
(while I keep yours)
you'll catch my breath

(I don't need air)

SELFISH SURVIVAL

Home has always been the sickness
of survival mode
where sacrifice is the same
as generosity
and sharing is careful
but now what is mine belongs to me
and while I know that
to share is to care
I am afraid to give in vain
after giving so much
I ended up
without shelter
and in a lot of pain

DREAMING IN POSSIBILITIES

Last night
I dreamed of peace
the same way a dog tries to run in their sleep
desperate for something
that isn't reality

WE DON'T HAVE TO SUFFER (LIKE THIS)

Our cycles don't always
have to be so long
we can choose to break them off
and create different
dimensions–I mean
directions

PASS THE JOY

When you feel joy
let it bleed
from eyes and ears
let everything you touch
and see
be littered with your happiness
let yourself be generous
with the resonance
of your glee

DOPPEL GANG

Why do we have the same favourite flower
and look our best in the same shade of yellow
why don't I know you
yet our freckles fall in the same patterns
we are symmetrical manifestations
on opposite sides of one really long equation
and the sum of it all is a probability unreal
so I will never meet you
but that doesn't mean
you aren't right here

YOU REMIND ME OF SOMEONE

You remind me
so much of my mom,
brother, stepsister, father
you remind me of me
when I'm not myself
you look like a friend I used to love
have we met?
you feel familiar
but with a name I've not heard of yet

CRUMBS OF CHILDHOOD

Little reminders of us
follow me
like mysterious shivers
and goose bumps that bring back memories
of those little moments of synchronicity
like saying something at the same time,
and then calling jinx
you owe me a pepsi

SLEEPOVERS

There is nothing like
sharing a twin bed
with a good friend and then
when the conversation naturally ends
we sigh our goodnights
and sink
into our sister slumbers

NEXT SUMMER

The last thing we said to each other
was something about plans for next summer
how we would meet in the middle
and then find our missing adventure
that was the last time we spoke
and now the months have taken over
our ever after
wherever your heart is now
I hope it beats faster

I still catch myself

reaching for your name

BURNT OUT, PLEASE HELP

And like that
like a winter chill snaps
your heart burnt out
and now you can't get it back
without someone to help
strike the match

GIVE AND TAKE

The dynamics of power

                             dictate

that you must give
if you want to take

so take all of me
and give me all of yours

I'll make strong
what is weak
as long as you
bring peace
to where
I am cursed

THIS LIFE IS BIGGER THAN IT SEEMS

Sometimes I don't know
if we are meant to be
because deep down I truly believe
that I am meant for everything
and we are just one thing
out of many

DAY BY DAY

I'm getting better
          slowly
in microscopic ways
that only my therapist
and partner can notice
not even I can see the change
but I will keep going
and start fresh everyday
do all the little things
that soothe my heart
and fuel my brain
while I try to remember
that I always work better
when I make time
          for play

YOU ARE THE ANSWER

The answer is: love

but isn't it always?
because to love is to respect
where the self ends
and reciprocate where
the other begins
every part played
by the same character
we blur the lines—
where do I start
why do you hide?
when love brought us here,
the gravity
of the collective mind,
the answer is: yes

you are the love
of my life

I love that
I don't have to explain,
you just know
when the subject
needs to change

RELATABLE

Write what you know
even if it's just overcast and sorrows
we've all felt the rain once or twice before
your pain is not unknown

FLOW

When I'm in a state of flow

I feel empty

I feel my heart fill and then drain
I feel like a visitor in my body
I feel like I am one and many
I feel like time is waiting for me
and I'm in no hurry

my hands type symphonies
as my mind taps into minds
when I write I cease to be me
and slowly become
a little bit of everyone
I have, and will never, meet

WELCOME BACK

Enough of these homes away from home
my broken bed calls
even though it squeaks and moans
it knows my bones
and I can't wait to come home

DARWIN IS DEAD

It's not at all
survival of the fittest

it's survival of the
kind & co-operative

don't buy it?
go ask man's best friend

life can't be a competition
if beasts can become friends

I think Darwin put us
on a dead end

UNION OF ONE

I will never be alone again
now that I have reunited
my soul with my skin
this is a partnership
until the death
and if one of us tries to quit
we will sink this ship
and find another vessel
to continue reigning the seasons

NOT ALONE TOGETHER

We are together alone
because first we are one
and then we become another
so we can never be
"alone together"
we have always been
together
and it is always temporary
when we are
alone

Together Alone

MUSHY LOVE

ALONE

SOME SPACE

Alone is a powerful place to be
so be wise with your power
and make the most
out of the precious privacy

ALONE WITH EVERYTHING

I want to be alone
so intimately
that the crack of sound breaking silence
breaks my heart and flushes my face
from cheeks to eyelids
so still and alone
inside this world of mine
outside the passage of time
singular and so connected
that by being
one
I eventually blend
into everything

ME AND THE CLOUDS USED TO HANG OUT

I have dreams of being
one with the sky
and rooted in the sea,
I have memories of being leaves,
falling in love,
and decomposing.
I have faint but fond daydreams
of my time as a butterfly and
when I made a living as a worm
turning the dead into fertility.
I have tainted but trusted reveries
of my lifetime as the first sunrise
and flashbacks of being the sea,
but now I forget how it feels
to have more than two feet,

WITH LOVE
inspired by Sharon Olds

I don't know how they do it with
so much love. The union of heart and soul
forever and maybe after
like colliding cosmic bodies bursting into
April showers, with mouths open and fingers
interlaced, skin so sweaty dripping with faith. The drum
of hearts synching, writing all those terrible love songs.
I don't know how they can get so close,
or why they would,
why would you give yourself away completely,
for free?
They are the Lovers I suppose, who love love so much
they make it everywhere they go
They feel so liberated doing it gently in the shower
and a little rougher on the couch.
exchanging saliva in domestic bliss
honey I'm home
give me a kiss

HAPPINESS IS REBELLIOUS

I recently learned the key to happiness
but if I tell you
you won't succeed
because the only way to be happy
is by doing your own thing
so don't listen to me—
rebel
immediately

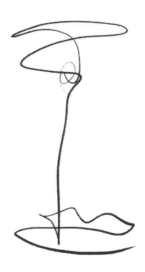

LITTLE HEART BIG FEELINGS

I'm sorry if this is a little
heart breaking
but I'm a little heart breaking
under the pressure I put myself under

life is a little raw
and I need to feel every degree
the good, the beautiful,
the disgusting

GROWTH AND PATIENCE

I'm doing the thing that
I promised
I would be better at
I'm trying not to
hate myself
I forgive my past,
my parents
I want
to move past all the habits
the coping mechanics
to find the root
of the rotten tree
I'll share the fruit
if you don't give up on me

SO MESSY

We missed our chance
to write a happy ending
met too soon,
gave up too early
we thought we had chapters left
that were part of a greater trilogy
but it turns out we were just scraps
ripped from a young girl's diary

FORGET ME

If you give me the gift
of forgiveness
then I beg you
please
grant me the blessing
of forgetting

CURSED AND UNSEEN

Invisibility is not a superpower
it is a curse
lived by those who are different
in appearance, mind, ability
disease and injury
over time it becomes a burden
too cumbersome to carry
and slowly it happens...

eventually you disappear
in all ways except literally

A DIFFERENT KIND OF BRAIN

Sometimes the words come out upside down
and no one knows
what I'm talking about
I sound fragmented—interrupting myself
with ideas out of
sequence
the sounds come out
but the meaning is long lost
in the meat behind my mouth

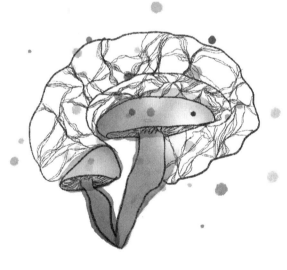

HEY HOW'S IT GOING?

Pretending not to be
not okay
who am I doing this for
why am I ignoring my pain
when I know very well that it's consuming
more and more of me everyday
I'm so tired of smiling
and lying
I need you to know
I'm going through something
and I need to do it alone
but I can't heal while
also playing this game
so next time you ask how I am
I'm going to shrug and say
I've had better days

ALL THIS EMPATHY

I hear the echo of my coping mechanisms,
drugs and deprivation
anything to dull the ripple effect
of this infectious infestation of media induced
mania—just more suits on monkeys
and right now I would rather be a fleshless zombie
than a healthy
                          feeling
human being
they don't feel anything and
I can't stomach all this empathy
I want to join the mindless
needless
and empty

Syrah Kai

TIME TO HOPE FOR THE BEST

We can't touch right now
but I hope you understand
how deeply I feel your heart within
we need to be alone for now
but I hope you don't forget
that while I think of you constantly
I need this time
to hope for the best

HOME FOR DINNER

I left home knowing
I had nowhere to go
knowing I would never be alone
I left my mother seeing that
I would soon become her
cutting cords that don't actually matter
because as long as I can smell
the winds of winter and moons of summer
I will always be a child
racing home for dinner

WHAT YOU SEE IS WHAT YOU DON'T

What you see
is the product of my solitary activities
my hermiting tendencies
my extraverted antisocial personality
becoming a butterfly at parties
then hiding in my room for a short eternity
because the show could not have gone on
if backstage wasn't always so busy
so enjoy the show and marvel
at my choreography
while it looks like a freestyle
this dance is something
I've spent years sculpting
out of bad teachers, eating disorders
depression, and men
just generally bothering me

PULLING AWAY

Reeling back the hooks
of my emotional attachments
I am coming home

HOW WAS YOUR WEEKEND?

Are we social creatures
or are we habits turned into dependency
do we really need each other
or are we putting up with our coworkers
because we fear vulnerability?

I sleep better alone

I like knowing you miss me

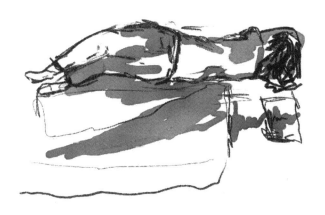

Syrah Kai

ADDICTED TO LONGING

There is no longing
with you
so do me a favor and leave
I can't wait to miss you

FLORAL WALLPAPER

Surrounded by the wrong people
they say my name
but don't notice that I'm not answering

PARANOID PROPAGANDA

We are social creatures
poisoned by a population
of social creepers
preying on the young and weak
buying and selling their spirits
using their bodies like raw meat
it's human nature to create communities
but how natural is stealing children
to be sold to the rich as perverted company
we are civilized until we get addicted
go broke and lose our minds
we are individuals to a point
but after that, what are we
but overly sentient zombies
so now how can I trust my neighbour
after watching all these youtube documentaries

FEAR OF FEAR

Fear is not a poisonous weapon
it is an instinct to run
to hide
to protect ourselves and our loves
don't misuse or misplace it
the feeling is just as valid
as hope and cheer
don't give in to the fear
of fear

Syrah Kai

NOT YOUR NEMESIS

I hated the way
he talked for hours
with his long winded storytelling
but I do the same

I cringed every time
she changed her mind
while mine changed
everyday

I judged their love
for being too new and uncommon
while all of my relationship were strange
in their own ways

I called her erratic
right before I lost my shit
thought they were all idiots
while I kept making
the exact same mistake

they felt too different to get close to
(because clearly we weren't the same)
yet my teachers made jokes about my
family name

I know I am not Narcissus
but maybe I'm his lost
half sister
obsessed with seeing the worst in myself,
like I see in others,
and unless I want to end up like my brother
maybe it's best
if I release the ego in my chest
and look the other way

STORYTELLER

Spend some time with me
and listen to the way I tell stories
the details I skip
the emotions I gloss over
and the moments I repeat over and over
open your heart and feel me
get a bit closer and you'll see
I'm lying through my teeth
I'm not this strong, hold me

Syrah Kai

I'M JUST VISITING

I'm an unwelcome visitor to homes
built on rigid traditional structure
because when I walk in
I warp and bend
values bound by gods and fathers
I peel back the skin of sheltered daughters
to reveal the truth of love
and limitations of family

I am an opened window
blinding unadjusted eyes
a killer of energy vampires
starving them of the naïveté and obedient belief
needed to find and herd sheep

I believe in nothing
but pray to it all
so when I come for dinner
get ready for the hierarchy to fall

COMING TRUE

I'm in a long distance relationship with my dreams
but I have a feeling we'll be together one day
something inside of me knows
there's a reason to believe

SOBBING

Sobbing
like spring
washing death away
unearthing the culprits of my suffering
it's hot
it's wet
and the salt doesn't taste bad
I like the way it stings— the way my belly heaves
I choke forgetting to breathe
it's a moment of eruption
a volcanic explosion
with all kinds of deep rooted debris
everything I kept in for so long
comes out singing in a way that sounds like sob
celebrating
finally
free

LITTLE BUDS OF HOPE

The trees are celebrating
just like I do
putting on a show
wearing every colour in my wardrobe
for once lighting up the room
before slowly receding back
to the shadows in my bed
resting in secret
until I blossom again

Syrah Kai

SECRETLY HAPPY

One day
I'll be sitting somewhere quaint
looking picturesque
wishing for a photo so I can share the moment
preserve the perfection
but instead
I'll just sip my drink
some wine or coffee,
and close my eyes and think:
I don't need you to know I'm happy

REST YOUR FLESH

Girl,
if you are putting in
all the work
you better be taking
all the breaks

seriously,
there is no stopping this clock
you've gotta keep the pace
I know you've got a dozen maps up your sleeve
and a million tricks to lead the way

but babe,
as a friend let me just say
I'm proud of you
but I also need you to take it easy today

hell,
call it quits
maybe it wasn't worth it anyway

because,
if you're going to work yourself rotten
it will always be a waste

BREAK FREE

When will you break
the choreography
and freestyle your heart
to happiness?

WALKING WHILE WOMAN

All I want
is to be able to go out alone
without having to walk fast
and avoid eye contact
I want to be able to run at 9pm
because that's when I feel the most powerful
but I know there are predators that lurk
and they aren't picky when it comes to dessert
they will take what they can get
and wrestle you for it
but I just want to run after work

WHEN YOUNG LOVE WAS PRETTY

I used to base my beauty on
how many times men harassed me
until I was old enough
to get angry
at them harassing
the new youth
like they did to me

my girl,
it's not your beauty they see
it's your young
ignorant
blank slate body
they want to drool all over
and make sticky

they know they can probably take it
without saying please
and what's more pleasing
is they know you wont fight back
because it just so happens that
you are the prettiest right before
you learn how

REPRESSED URGES

How about we flex free will
and decide to enjoy our reproductive beauty
in other productive ways
new strategy ladies:
do whatever you want
and don't worry about not passing on your blood
or someone else's name
pass on in peace
the world is hardly deserving anymore, anyway

GONE LIKE THAT

Something separated us
and I can't get a grasp on its permanence
it's like you've floated away
all while screaming
that you'll be right back
and I don't really know
if I believe that

IT WAS TIME TO GO

The last of your things
and you have left
but the emptiness and dust
left behind
drove me outside
into the relentless rain
the sun was sick again
I walked around dazed
unsure of where to go
I wandered until I found myself
at the edge of the ocean
who cooed my name
it sounded like my mother
so I sat in her wetness to weep my sadness
finally letting my tears go home

Syrah Kai

THIS BELONGS TO YOU

You left some of your skin cells
on my side table
I guess you forgot to take them with you
your hair is here too
and the oil your body produced
that made you smell like a memory
one I don't want to be reintroduced to
I want the real you

187

WHY DIDN'T YOU

When that little voice in your heart begged
you didn't listen

why didn't you?

what about me
wasn't worth the honesty

why didn't you?

how long could you have gone
without telling me

why did you?

Syrah Kai

CAN YOU KEEP (ME) A SECRET?

Secrets don't have parties

they don't have friends

secrets stay locked away

and forgotten

the life of a secret

is that of a bucket

catching leaky pipes in the basement

you are my best kept secret

and I plan on keeping it

NO BEST FRIENDS

I have a bad case
of best friend syndrome
I can't get close with anyone
even though we haven't been close for years
even though we never will be again
I keep trying to recreate our bond
in the midnight chambers
 of my heart

CURIOUS AT MOST

I made you curious
                at most

but you didn't want to be
unconditionally engulfed
and adored
            by me

and even though it was crushing
and gave me chalk for bones
I'm sorry I tried to make you
                        my home

AN OIL PAINTING CALLED "THE LAST LOOK"

I wish I knew
when the last time was coming
so I could hug you for a proper minute
and engrave you into my brain
a museum of cave drawings
your eyes forever encased
behind plexiglass and laser beams
so no one can take
your last loving gaze
away from me

Syrah Kai

WE SAID GOODBYE THIS TIME

My last memory of us was too painful
I had to make one up
so it wouldn't hurt so much to think about you

WITH & WITHOUT

Would you rather be alone with yourself
or alone surrounded by others
one feels like a choice made by philosophers
and authors
while the other feels like a fool's attempt at acceptance
that ends with the anxiety of a wallflower

Syrah Kai

VOYEURISTIC

I'm always alone
when I catch the best sunsets
always by accident
always majestic
alone to embrace it
watching the sorbet hues infuse
like an intimate relationship
it feels a lot like magic
and a little voyeuristic
me, alone
watching the sunset

NOVEMBER NIGHTS

Midnight meditations
spent trying to astral project my heart
into a different existence
a different soul
in a lifeform completely unknown
what's out there beyond the skyline of starlights,
the expansive void, the longest shadow
surrounded by the warmth of my awareness
I hear the cold call of saturn and tremors of pluto
sitting on the moon in my mind
drifting in and out of my fragile sense of time
I have never been here before
but it feels like home

YOU'RE TOO KIND

Some people prefer to see you down
it makes them feel better
about themselves
because in their minds
they are the hero that helped
but once you rise
their love will suddenly underwhelm
until the next time you stumble
when you'll notice they only smiled
becasue you fell

FEELING THE SPECTRUM

I'm coming to terms with the idea
that emotions are not signs of weakness
that there are more nuanced feelings
in between excruciating joy
and rage that is seething
that anxiety can be a fire alarm out of battery
that goes off constantly
that guilt can't be proven if it's not real
that nostalgia is tragic
that love isn't always manic
I'm learning to give myself permission to feel
and I'm inviting heart to feel it all with me

KRONENBERG

metamorphosis is ugly
don't let poetry trick you otherwise

TOO MUCH FOR ONE HEART

I'm cursed

I'll never be able
to make someone
truly feel
how I love
it's too much

NEEDY

you need me most

when I need

to be

alone

you make me

look so cold

SEE THROUGH

Your eyes always looked away
too quickly
to subdue me
you tried to tell me stories
but the truth fell from your face
and gave you away

I USED TO COME HOME TO YOU

I came home
and accidentally looked for you
because your eyes used to always find mine
and your face used to light up with smiles
because you knew I would always come home
with a story and a surprise

BULLIES

Bullies & bitches
I grew up collecting whispers
like eyebrow stitches
with hair that curled sporadically
and a delayed femininity
there was a target on my back
the moment I turned 13

LEAVE YOUR HOMETOWN

they say growth happens
outside your comfort zone

well

I've never been this
far away from home

ME IN THE MIRROR

I got drunk alone and never loved myself more
never saw such sweetness
in the intricacies of my body
let them judge
while I pour another glass
of my favourite deep red
they don't know what they are missing
and I plan on keeping it that way
all this is vip
just me for me

ONE OF A KIND

The wind heard you cry
asking

"why am I one of a kind
when I could be so much happier
blending in with others
instead they stare at the way I wear my hair
the way my eyes cut corners
they touch me out of curiosity
they ask how it happened
and if I would do it over"

eventually the wind replied
in a mountainous sigh

I've seen the world from dust to ocean
I've met every umbrella that fought to stay open
I've seen the many, and the more
but I've never seen anything
so fluid and formed
as the colour of your voice before

THE AUDACITY

Teach me to be brave
and brazen
so I can have the courage to ask
for what I want
and the audacity to expect it

THE COURAGE

I am growing the courage it takes
to be bold and blatant
so my visions may come to life
exactly as I see them

LEAVE ME BE

I am not to be picked
or pruned

I am not to be flattered
or swooned

I am on a mission
and you are not my guru

THE WORK IS SILENT

There are dreams in us
that can't be translated
goals we can't articulate
visions so grand
words will only cause others
to misunderstand

I wish I could express the fire I feel
for the passions I hold close
but what I call a mountain
to you might look like a hill

but alas this is the work
that takes place within
we must do it alone
until we can share
what we have built

THE GODS KNOW WHERE TO FIND ME

The gods know where to find me
when I can't get the wind out of my hair
driving up these curly highways she keeps taking me down
where the mountains go from rock to sand
and my ocean in the passenger seat
stares out the window admiring her masterpiece

I have visions like white caps
frothing with mythology
spoken into form
the present packaged perfectly
falling into my lap
on my way to a happenstance party

the gods know where to find me
at a symposium of the senses
where the conversation is louder
than the music
but the band still plays us a symphony

the clatter and splashes of life lessons
and memories
keep us warm under the nightshade
of palm trees
wrapped in cashmere and outdoor heating
hands will be held
and cheeks will bump cheeks

as mountains melts into beach
and my ocean still watches her masterpiece
while the flames flirt with the breeze
I know the wind is coming
she just RSVP'd
and the gods?
they know where to find me

ALONE IN NATURE

Out here I feel more myself
but less human
less of a person
and more of a joyous existence

GEODE

Prismatic dreamscapes
hidden away
in old warts made of stone
hoping to stay untouched
by the man who judges
alone

GAINING PERSPECTIVE

I don't know if I'm doing the right thing or not
I don't know what's right anymore at all
there's a sense of foreboding that repels me
from following instructions
something inside me tells me
to keep going forward
through dense untamed forest
that shelter will be found
with or without a degree—or my parents' help
I'm falling behind but I can still see the pack
following each other down the beaten path
but from my vantage
I can see where they will eventually bottleneck
and will have to trample each other
to get to the other side
so I stay low, stay solo
and keep trekking on to find
the blooming butterfly meadow
I've only seen as flashes in my mind

DIZZY

This is what the world does
it spins and spins
in and out
of control
so we hold on tight
along for the ride
trying our best not to hurl

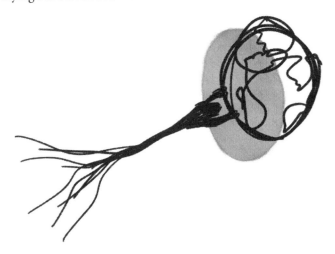

Syrah Kai

EASY GO

Everyone leaves
they have to
when there are more reasons to go
than to stay
everyone has somewhere to be
and I can't join in
it's not my time
even if it kills me to say goodbye
and it serves me right
for investing anything in anyone
when I could lose it all over night

NO ONE KNOWS LOSS

No one knows loss
until they are stolen from

until they lose something irreplaceable
something one of a kind
once in a lifetime
hand made and given away

something old that fits like new
something deep and secure
something that got sick with something
that has no cure

no one knows loss
                        until they lose

FLUSHED NO MATTER WHAT

Don't worry
I'm not taking risks with you
I'm playing these cards in my favour
hurt me and I will flourish
love me and I will live forever

STAY IN THE MINORITY

Most people—

(your family,
your neighbors,
the people who live within your national borders,)

most people—
play it safe
by the rules
they fear change
and worship the status quo

don't be most people
be entirely and firmly very much your own
don't let the pressure of most people
prune your soul

ATTENTION DEFICIT

Comforted by natural light and big blankets
I slipped back into my body
to feel this moment
for what it is:
a chance to submit to stillness
so I stay and watch the rain play
and resist my urges
to check notifications or fidget

MY BODY

My body remembers everything
rough and mild
every angry face
after I declined a smile
every grubby finger nail
undeserving
every sandy tongue
that pushed its way through my teeth
my body remembers everything
and now some parts of me
are too sensitive to sensitivity
because the roughness
remembers my body

WHO CRIES

They cry:

lies!

she tells lies
she wants to manipulate
so she employs her cries

TRICKSTERS DON'T TRUST

I don't trust
easily or well
because I've been
deceived by many devils
that first came off
as angels

NOTHING MATTERS, SO

I'm done being angry

all I want is to
live my true story
without a million rhetorics forming

I want to present the facts
of my experience
tell you to take it
with a little salt and pepper
because I don't believe in added sugar

and maybe I don't know
all that much better
but I know where I've been
and how I've been treated
and for a while
it felt a little too fucking different

like it was my fault for the inconvenience
like this was skin I chose to live in
like I had any say in the matter
of my birth religion

well I sold all my gold
and now I pray to nothing
because at the heart of it all
that's all we are
and I find that exhilerating

Together Alone

so when I pray to it all
(and the nothing in between)
I ask for just
this one thing

for you to be you
and me to be me

without a million rhetorics forming

PLAY THAT BACK

In the middle of the night
long after sleep stuck its tongue out at me
episodes of life
marathon randomly
and suddenly I can't stop the replay
of indirect selfishness
and misunderstandings
stuck in a loop of embarrassment
no matter how much I try
how tight I squeeze my eyes
I seem to regret the little things
more than all the wasted time

NO YANG

What can you say about pleasure
if you can't recount pain
you don't know how to savour
when you have had no thirst to quench
and no hunger to pang
what keeps you striving
when all your needs are satisfied
before they have a chance
to call your name
you're all yin, no yang

SCAR TISSUE

I'm nagged with the memory
of how quickly we connected
the gravity of our attraction
the magnitude
the distraction
of the push and pull
transaction
I'll never forget
how we happened
slow and then instant
we burned ourselves in passion

THE PLEASURE IS ALL MINE

Late night self love
I lay back and dream of
your forbidden touch

from the safety of my fingertips
I taste what I am afraid
to initiate

I wish you could watch
but you'll only want to take over
and this is my pleasure
I own her

YOU ARE THE ANSWER

You don't need validation from authority
or any system
to know if you're going in the right direction
that must come from within
because on the outside
we can't always tell
who means well
and who means they want
a little something something
so trust yourself

ON THE ROAD

Loneliness is the path it takes
to get to your goals
it's a road best walked
head high and alone
because who you are
when you set out to conquer the world
won't be the same person
who sits on the throne

I FEEL SO TRAPPED
IN A BODY
THAT EVERYONE
CAN SEE

UNSPOKEN

Don't believe in me
because I don't want
to let you down

I don't want to know
what you see in me
because I might see
something different entirely

and the beauty of potential
is that it can turn into
anything

so let me unfold
organically

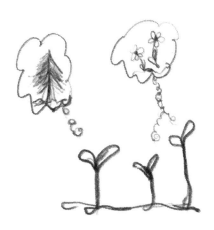

UNLOCKED

I am not potential
locked away
I am the actualization
of what happens when
the wind carries a dandelion
to a field of poppies
I didn't choose to come here
and I will not change to stay
I am not potential
I am what I am
and so I became

LESSONS LEARNED

Lone wolves
may not tell many stories
but they can teach you
a solid lesson or two

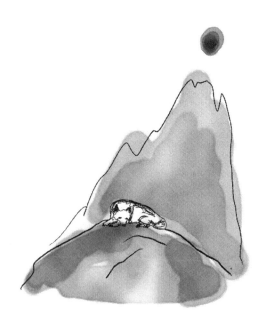

NOW YOU SEE ME

I was not seen
I was misinterpreted
by old eyes that wanted to own
the parts of me
I had yet to reconcile

I was not heard
I was interrupted
with rude abruption
cut off mid sentence
re-explained with
pedantic instructions

I was not felt, really
when they touched and teased me
coming close
only to see right through
the best parts of me
but I see

I am not what you want
I am what you think you need
because bless your mother
but she alone couldn't teach you
how to love women properly
in a world that still prefers
that they stay pretty
yet unseen

THE DELUSIONS OF ANXIETY

The gravity in my chest expanded and took over
absorbing every thought and memory
turning them into complicated conspiracy theories
I swear there is a deeper meaning
this isn't what it seems

PANIC AND AGONY

Neither here
nor there—I am
thrown out
side of reality
smacking into catastrophe
panic sweating
and clammy I fear
that if I can't catch my breath
I'll never stop spinning

BLEEDING FROM MY HEADPHONES

There's a certain kind of music
that always tastes better alone
those awkward shy lyricists
with bedroom voices that taste like velvet
know just how to make my heart explode
there's a specific hour of midnight
that opens up a hole into another dimension
where the world stands still
and it's finally safe for my thoughts to race
and emotions to pour over
without the risk of leaving stains

NEVER ENOUGH TIME OUT

Sometimes all I want
is something burgundy
to sip on
and absolutely no one
wasting my time
that's the dream life

I AM A ROCK

If I can't be an island
then I shall become a hill
not entirely cut off
                    from people
                    and places
but a trek to get to
so only the worthy will

CROSS THE LINE ONE MORE TIME

If you cannot accept
the terms of my bounduries
then we will never

be at peace

(don't push me)

TAKE ME TO THE SEA

The clashing of the world
disturbs my inner peace
all roads lead to traffic
while my heart gives birth
to olive trees

Syrah Kai

NO GOING BACK

Homesick in my soul
but
where I'm from
is not
where I belong

CARRYING ON

Endurance
looks like

running up stairs
for fun
but also

carrying on
when there's nothing
carrying you

SAD AND ABSURD

My sadness
looks like sleeping too much
and not eating properly
it feels like I have water in my ears
making the world sound blurry
it tastes like metal
and smells like forgotten laundry
my sadness is a recluse
do not disturb
collecting dust
choking on words
my sadness can't remember
the last time life
wasn't absurd

WHY THE WRITER WRITES

When I was young
I used to leave
a pen and paper
out at night
and prayed for god
to write back to me

I never got the message

but ever since then
I haven't stopped writing

message received

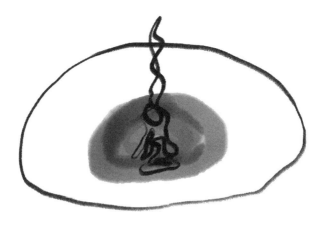

Syrah Kai

A DREAM WITH NO MEANING

There is no one else to live for
there is only you in your skin
and fists in your pockets
wondering
if it will be like this forever
or if something magical will show up
and make this all seem like a stupid dream
that didn't mean anything

EXHALE

The tide exhales
revealing death on the beach
beautiful skeletons
and evicted homes
catch the light
and call to me
so I scan and collect
the most brightly coloured
death beds
thinking how I can glue them to mirrors
or collect them in shoeboxes
and stash them forever untouched
beneath my dread

ALONE TO KNOW

Being alone is the only way to know
if these voices are mine
or thoughts I've been sold

COOKIES

Crying just doesn't do it for me like it used to
there's no release
just irritated sinuses
and hours of sniffing
letting go and letting it out–I don't know how
I can whimper
but then I just sit there and freeze
stuck in a mud pit of sick sadness and heavy grief
but this is mine to carry
so instead of spending so much energy
trying to feel things
maybe there is a way I can untangle this web
and find my way out rationally
but first,
a box of cookies

Syrah Kai

TIME KILLS EVERYTHING

Don't go on
ignoring the pain
treat your broken spirits and passions
because while time can heal all wounds
it can also fester infections

THE DRUMS OF CHANGE

Do you feel that
rushing
through your veins,
that's not blood
that's change

you are driven by a force
called love
but that's not your heart
beating
it's the ceremonial drums

IF I FALL
IN LOVE
WITH MYSELF
I BETTER
TREAT ME RIGHT

SUPER SENSITIVE

Empathy is both a super power and a burden
people expect the world
from you,
inside you
to open at a moment's notice
but this shoulder is mine
and it's mine first
I understand that you need a safe place
to cry
but I also need a lot of my own time
so these are my boundaries
and I need you
to find some strength in yourself
or please wait in queue

TALKING TO MYSELF

One time I talked to myself
like I talk to others
and cried
I was so kind

CHRONIC LOW GRADE ANXIETY

She can't eat
with tidal waves crashing
pushing
her heartbeat underwater

she can't see
the smoke from the silver linings
the differences between her mind
and her anxiety

she can't breathe
it's all too shallow
she lost her sleep a long time ago
it was stolen by the grabby hands
that hide in the shadows

I'M IN SEASON

Polka dots are back in season
between my legs
where my thighs keep meeting
it must be important
because they keep screaming
pink and red
rash decisions

LOVING MYSELF AS IF I'M SOMEONE ELSE

I am learning to take care of myself
as if I'm someone else

because my pets only get
the best food I can afford

and my friends all receive
immense quality of support

my mother never cries alone
and my lover always gets the most

and if I ever gave any less
it would tear my own heart apart

so this is the start of taking care of myself
as if I am someone else

because I want to be treated
with just as much heart

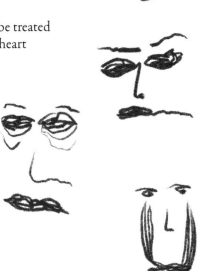

LONELY KIND OF LOUD

I love the sounds of solitude
of teengers practing playing the flute
knuckles cracking as writers rush to get the words out
I can't get enough of this lonely kind of loud
the solo soul searching of meditative bodies
humming along to a collective strumming
this is the stillness I seek
the self reflection that happens
during late afternoons
or so-late-it's-early mornings

WITH A CLUTTERED HEART

My heart is littered
with crossed out scribbles
names of boys and fingerprints of girls
people who have crossed me
that revenge is not worth
my heart is in the closet
where I keep my favourite secrets
like journals I have yet to burn
and albums that prove
I used to be young and lovely

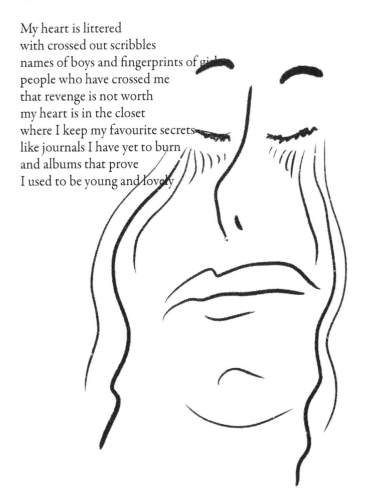

BETTER ALONE THAN ABANDONED

My fear of abandonment
isn't a fear of being alone

I know alone

and alone doesn't leave me
in the middle of the night
after trashing our hotel room
after going through my phone

alone doesn't threaten
to throw me to the curb
and replace me in a day

being alone is fine
it's the sudden ripping apart
of my trust and heart
that shocks my nerves into thinking

I needed to beg you to stay

DO YOU MISS ME TONIGHT?

Did I slip into your mind
on those lonesome nights
that plagued your early thirties?

Did I leave my fingerprints behind
and did you not even try to erase them?
I'm sorry I left my traces
but you know we were something crazy
in all the unbelievable ways
I know you loved me

but this isn't the kind of story you tell just anybody
the attention would only salt the heartbreak
and I know you're trying so hard to let go

but I bet you can't help but reminisce
when the moon hangs just like this
do you ever look up and wish
I never slipped away?

NEVER LOVED YOU

There's a place in hell
for people like you
it's called
I never loved you

GIVE GIVE GIVE, TAKE BACK

If they won't reciprocate
I won't dedicate
it's as simple as that

so take what you want
but don't be surprised
if I ask for it back

THE BEST OF THE WORST

Seeing the best in someone
who only makes you feel the worst
is probably the worst
thing you can do to yourself

would you close your eyes and play with knives?

why pretend you can change them
the best is a lot better than this
better will come

MAKE IT WORTH FORGETTING

Be intentional and precise
be kind but move on
be firm but loosen your grip
unless you want to leave bruises

don't settle for the unspoken
turn around and keep going
the morning will come again
and so it goes,

another chapter for the story

HIDDEN

You'll never know
what it's like to be alone
until you have to keep a secret
that if told
could seriously hurt someone you love
by no fault of your own

YOU & ME

I have discovered what's worth
rediscovering
it's not about the work
it's about the energy
where I put my heart
is where my love bleeds
I've discovered the truth
is liberating
I've rediscovered the you
in me

Syrah Kai

AND SO IT STILL GOES

I was quick to leave home
but have only spent my time ever since
trying to recreate it
with only a few improvements

BE ALL KINDS OF EVERYTHING

There is nothing–I repeat nothing
out there
in space or ocean
nothing in the countries where other languages are spoken
nothing in the desert
and absolutely nothing at the top of the rockies
that isn't already in you
you are absolutely and infinitely everything
but you wont believe it until you are broken wide open
so be broken
be everything

Syrah Kai

WORDS WORTH FEELING

Writing is an exercise
in detached empathy
it is the practice
of connecting so deeply
you take on others' pain
experiences
and memories
and then rearrange them into words
      worth reading
      worth feeling
      worth remembering

FORGIVEN

I forgive myself

finally

because I know next time
I'll do it differently

Syrah Kai

Together Alone

Syrah Kai

Together Alone

Made in the USA
Columbia, SC
17 February 2022

56400200R00152